Celebrations in My World

Canada Day

Molly
Aloian

Crabtree Publishing Company
www.crabtreebooks.com

Crabtree Publishing Company

www.crabtreebooks.com

Author: Molly Aloian
Coordinating editor: Chester Fisher
Series and project editor: Penny Dowdy
Editor: Adrianna Morganelli
Proofreader: Crystal Sikkens
Editorial director: Kathy Middleton
Production coordinator: Katherine Berti
Prepress technician: Katherine Berti
Project manager: Kumar Kunal (Q2AMEDIA)
Art direction: Dibakar Acharjee (Q2AMEDIA)
Cover design: Tarang Saggar (Q2AMEDIA)
Design: Neha Kaul (Q2AMEDIA)
Photo research: Farheen Aadil (Q2AMEDIA)

Photographs:
Abdallahh: p. 13
Alamy: Hemis: p. 12; Yvon Sauvé: p. 17; Vespasian: p. 28
Associated Press: Jonathan Hayward: front cover,
    Dave Martin: p. 26; Jerry S. Mendoza: p. 23
BigStockPhoto: Rusak: p. 4
Confederation Life Gallery of Canadian History: p. 8
Corbis: Bettmann: p. 9; Paul A. Souders: p. 18;
    Rudy Sulgan: p. 15
Creative Comments: p. 5
Dreamstime: p. 25 (bottom); Pixart: p. 19
Stephanie Fysh: p. 14
Getty Images: Keith Douglas: p. 24, 31; Jack Fletcher: p. 6;
    Donald Weber: p. 27
Jupiter Images: Radius Images: p. 1
Photolibrary: Garry Black/All Canada Photos: p. 16;
    Rob Crandall: p. 11; George Hunter/Superstock: p. 21
Reuters: Shaun Best: p. 22; Chris Helgren: p. 29;
    Jim Young: p. 20
Shutterstock: Gencay M. Emin: p. 30; Stephen Finn: p. 10;
    Andrew Olscher: p. 25 (top)
Travel-Images: R. Eime: p. 7

Library and Archives Canada Cataloguing in Publication

Aloian, Molly
    Canada Day / Molly Aloian.

(Celebrations in my world)
Includes index.
ISBN 978-0-7787-4752-9 (bound).--ISBN 978-0-7787-4770-3 (pbk.)

    1. Canada Day--Juvenile literature. 2. Canada Day--History--Juvenile
literature. I. Title. II. Series: Celebrations in my world

FC503.C3A46 2010   j394.263   C2009-902025-4

Library of Congress Cataloging-in-Publication Data

Aloian, Molly.
    Canada Day / Molly Aloian.
        p. cm. -- (Celebrations in my world)
    Includes index.
    ISBN 978-0-7787-4770-3 (pbk. : alk. paper) -- ISBN 978-0-7787-4752-9
(reinforced library binding : alk. paper)
    1. Canada Day--Juvenile literature. I. Title. II. Series.

F1033.A47 2010
394.2630973--dc22

                                2009014150

5549

Crabtree Publishing Company

www.crabtreebooks.com   1-800-387-7650

Published in Canada
Crabtree Publishing
616 Welland Ave.
St. Catharines, ON
L2M 5V6

Published in the United States
Crabtree Publishing
PMB16A
350 Fifth Ave., Suite 3308
New York, NY 10118

Published in the United Kingdom
Crabtree Publishing
White Cross Mills
High Town, Lancaster
LA1 4XS

Published in Australia
Crabtree Publishing
386 Mt. Alexander Rd.
Ascot Vale (Melbourne)
VIC 3032

Contents

What is Canada Day?

Canada Day is a holiday. It celebrates Canada's birthday, July 1. Canada is a country in North America that **borders** the United Sates. Canada has ten **provinces** and three **territories**.

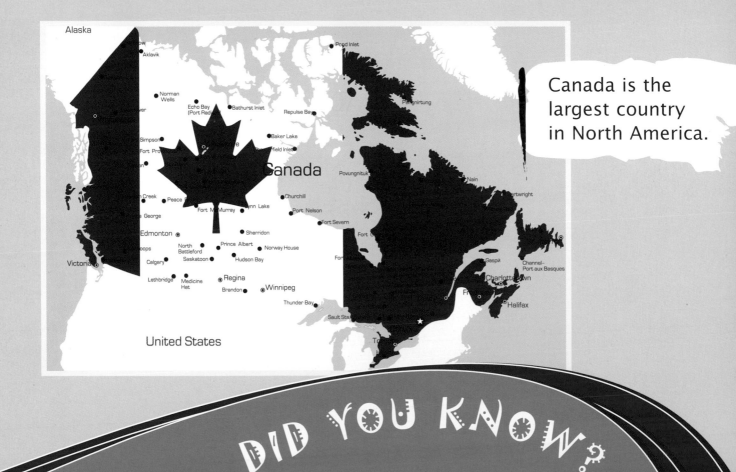

Canada is the largest country in North America.

DID YOU KNOW?

Canada Day is celebrated on July 1 every year. When July 1 falls on a Sunday, Canadians celebrate on Monday.

4

Canadians of all ages celebrate Canada Day.

Canada Day is a **statutory** holiday. Most Canadians get the day off work or school. Government offices and businesses close. Families and communities gather to celebrate.

First Canadians

People have lived in Canada for thousands of years. Some are called First Nations people. There are many different First Nations, such as Cree, Blackfoot, and Okanagan peoples. They live all across Canada. Each group speaks a different language and has different **traditions**.

First Nations families were some of the first people to live in Canada.

DID YOU KNOW?

Explorers from Europe discovered Canada in 1497. People from Britain and France claimed the land for their own. They formed colonies in Eastern Canada.

Many Inuit families live in Canada's colder climates.

Inuit peoples have lived in the **Arctic** region of Canada for over a thousand years. They live in the Northwest Territories, Nunavut, and Yukon. Inuit means "the people."

Dominion of Canada

On July 1, 1867, four provinces signed the Constitution Act of 1867. Nova Scotia, New Brunswick, Ontario, and Quebec became the Dominion of Canada. A dominion is land ruled by another country. Canada was ruled by Britain.

Representatives from each province agree to become a Dominion.

DID YOU KNOW?

From 1867 to 1982 Canada Day was called Dominion Day.

Britain's Queen Elizabeth and Canada's Prime Minister Pierre Trudeau signed Canada's new Constitution Act.

More provinces and territories—British Columbia, Saskatchewan, Alberta, Manitoba, Prince Edward Island, Newfoundland, Nunavut, Northwest Territories, and Yukon—joined later.

In 1982, Canada signed a new Constitution Act. This officially made Canada an **independent** country.

9

Two Languages

• This stop sign in Ottawa is in French and English.

Canada is a **bilingual** country. Bilingual means two languages. Europeans who moved to Canada in the 1700s spoke French or English. Today, Canada's official languages are also English and French. Canada's leaders and some government offices use both languages. Products are labeled in English and French.

DID YOU KNOW?

French-speaking Canadians call Canada Day "Fête du Canada." In English this means "to celebrate Canada."

10

Quebec was settled by the French, and most people still speak French there today.

Not all Canadians speak both languages. Most speak English. In the province of Quebec, most people speak French. Laws in Canada help French-speaking people protect their **culture**.

11

Many Cultures

Canada is a multicultural country. Multicultural means "many cultures." In the 1900s, Canada wanted people to **immigrate**, or move, to its country. It offered immigrants cheap land in the western areas of Canada.

People with many backgrounds make Canada their home.

DID YOU KNOW?

Canada made a law to protect its many cultures. The Multiculturalism Act of 1988 makes sure that every Canadian can celebrate their culture.

Many people celebrate their cultural background on Canada Day.

Many people moved to Canada. They came from countries such as China, Russia, Cuba, and the United States. Canadians honor their home country as well as where they came from.

New Citizens

Every year about 150,000 people move to Canada to become citizens. A citizen is a person who belongs to a country. Canadian citizens obey laws and respect the **rights** of other Canadians. In return they are given freedoms and rights.

Television crews and officials congratulate new Canadian citizens.

DID YOU KNOW?

On Canada Day, the government holds special citizenship ceremonies throughout the country to make new immigrants Canadian citizens.

14

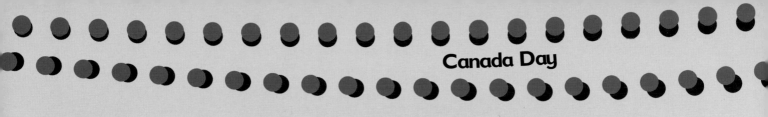

Some people come to Canada to attend college.

Some people move to Canada to join other family members who live there. Others come to study at Canadian schools or work at jobs. Some people move to escape danger in their own country.

15

Canada Day in Ottawa

Ottawa, in Ontario, is the capital, or most important city, in Canada. Canada's Parliament buildings are in Ottawa. The Parliament buildings are where the country's laws are made. The biggest Canada Day celebration happens in Ottawa every year.

Ottawa holds the largest Canada Day celebration in the country.

DID YOU KNOW?

Hundreds of thousands of people gather in Ottawa for the Canada Day celebrations.

July 1 in Ottawa begins with a flag-raising ceremony and a parade with music and military **drills**. The Prime Minister, the leader of Canada, makes a speech. People take part in games and races. Different cultures hold events that celebrate their traditions. People enjoy concerts, too!

Team Canada plays a game of hockey on Parliament Hill to celebrate Canada Day.

Mounties

The Royal Canadian Mounted Police (RCMP) perform a Musical Ride in Ottawa every year on Canada Day. The RCMP is Canada's **national** police force. An RCMP officer is called a Mountie.

A Mountie wears a bright red jacket and black pants with a yellow stripe.

A Mountie and his horse train for the Musical Ride on Canada Day.

Thirty-two riders on horses perform the Musical Ride. Riders and horses practice for months on routines and drills. It is almost like a dance for a rider and his horse.

Thirty-two RCMP officers and their horses perform the Musical Ride.

DID YOU KNOW?

All RCMP horses are black. There are about one hundred horses specially raised by Canada's police force.

19

Look Up in the Sky!

Look up—there's a lot to see in the sky during Canada Day. The Snowbirds are a nine-plane team of Canadian Air Force pilots. Every year they put on a Canada Day air show in Ottawa. They do special stunts and make patterns while flying their planes.

The Snowbirds fly over the Parliament building on Canada Day.

DID YOU KNOW?

The Snowbirds are known as Warriors of the Air. They have been performing air shows since 1971.

Cities, such as Ottawa, hold fireworks displays on Canada Day.

At nighttime, many Canadian cities hold fireworks displays. Fireworks shoot high into the air and explode in huge, colored flashes. Ottawa has one of the biggest fireworks displays in Canada.

21

Other Celebrations

Communities celebrate with picnics, parades, concerts, fireworks, and other events. In Halifax people begin with a pancake breakfast. The annual Canada Day parade in Montreal celebrates the many cultures of that city.

On Canada Day many communities hold parades.

DID YOU KNOW?

On Canada Day in Newfoundland, people hold a Memorial Day to remember the soldiers who fought and died in the First World War.

22

Border cities celebrate Canada Day and Independence Day in a four-day long celebration.

Canada Day falls close to the American Independence Day on July 4. Many cities close to the Canadian-American border get together and celebrate a four-day long festival that marks both holidays.

23

The Canadian Flag

Canada's flag is red and white with a red maple leaf in the middle. It became Canada's official flag in 1965. Many Canadians dress in red and white on Canada Day.

The red maple leaf is a **symbol** for Canada.

DID YOU KNOW?

On Canada Day many people show pride in their country by flying the Canadian flag. Painting a red maple leaf on your face is also popular.

24

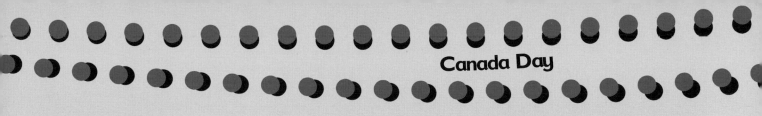

Canadians display the
flag on Canada Day.

The maple leaf has been a
Canadian symbol since the
1700s. First Nations people
discovered that maple sap
could be used for food. Later,
it became the national symbol
of Canada. It is on the Canadian
flag and the Canadian penny.

Canadian
penny

Canada Day Music

How do Canadians wish happy birthday to their country? They sing their national anthem, or song, "O, Canada."

"O, Canada" is the Canadian national anthem.

DID YOU KNOW?

"O, Canada" was first performed in French on June 24, 1880. It was made Canada's national anthem almost a hundred years later, in 1980.

In Halifax, Nova Scotia, people start Canada Day celebrations by gathering to sing "O, Canada" outside of a historic fort called Citadel Hill. In Vancouver, British Columbia, they hold an annual "O, Canada" singing contest.

Many Canadian musicians and bands perform their music at Canada Day concerts held across the country.

The Canadian band Blue Rodeo performs a concert on Canada Day.

Canada Day Food

Canada Day is celebrated in the middle of summer. An outdoor picnic or barbecue is a popular way for Canadians to celebrate.

July 1 falls in the middle of summer when the weather is warm.

DID YOU KNOW?

A pancake breakfast with maple syrup is also popular on Canada Day. About 85 percent of the world's maple syrup comes from Canada.

Local politicians and new citizens get the honor of making the first cut.

Most birthday parties have cakes. Canada's birthday party has them, too. Many communities celebrate Canada Day by sharing a birthday cake during the festivities.

In Medicine Hat, Alberta, people enter the annual Canada Day cake baking and decorating contest. After the best cakes are awarded, they are cut and served to people at the event.

Canada Day Quiz

1. What does Canada Day celebrate?
2. What was Canada Day called before 1982?
3. Who were the first Canadians?
4. What color are all RCMP horses?
5. What is Canada's national symbol that is found on the Canadian flag?

DID YOU KNOW?

Canada is the largest country in North America, and the second-largest country in the world. Over 33 million people live in Canada.

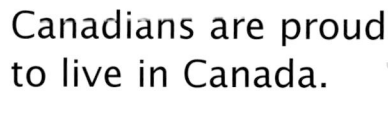

Canadians are proud
to live in Canada.

Answers:
1. Canada's birthday
2. Dominion Day
3. First Nations and Inuit peoples
4. black
5. the maple leaf

Glossary

Arctic The northern polar region of Earth

bilingual Two different languages

border A line that separates two countries

colony An area where people move to that is ruled by another country

culture The beliefs and habits of a group of people

drills Training a group to do military movements

immigrate To move to another country to live

independent Having control over your own rules and laws

national Relating to one country

province A set area of land that makes some of their own laws

rights The freedoms and protections allowed to members of a country

statutory Something that everyone must do because it is a law

symbol Something that stands for something else

territory A set area of land ruled by the federal government

tradition Customs or beliefs handed down from one generation to another

Index

Printed in China—CT